Diet recommendations for TCM - Liver - Moist heat in the liver and gallbladder

Please check these recommendations always with a TCM nutrition consultant, therapist, doctor or dietician. The recipes and the list of ingredients are supporting also the conventional medical therapy. The calorie disclosures of fresh ingredients (fruit and vegetables) vary according to quality and time of harvest. The contents were checked by a dietician and a nutrition consultant for the Traditional Chinese Medicine (TCM).

Author:
©2017 Josef Miligui
www.ebns.at

Source:
The lists are created from the EBNS database for nutritional counseling. The database is used by dietitians, therapists and doctors for advising the patient / client.

Literature:
The specialist literature and the training documents of the German and Austrian dietary and traditional Chinese medicine serve as a knowledge base. We have used the documents as a basis of knowledge, adapted it to our experience and completed them.
http://di-book.com

Title Photo:
©2008 Erika Weixlbaumer

Production and publishing:
BoD – Books on Demand, Norderstedt
ISBN: 9783752858518

Diet recommendations for TCM - Liver - Moist heat in the liver and gallbladder

1 Treatment strategy

Release moisture and heat, move qi into the middle, strengthen spleen. Hot NO, warm LITTLE / NO, neutral / refreshing YES (sour LITTLE), cold and bitter YES, else NO

2 Avoid

Too much alcohol, denatured food, frozen food, fast food, late food, coffee, sugar, raw foods, dairy products, greasy, fried, cheese-baked, too much eggs, lamb, hot spices, too salty - combination of: sweet-fat, salty fat

3 Breakfast

	kkal. per serving
Adzuki Bean and Rice Soup	199
Barley soup	265
Barley water	44
Carrot and rice gruel soup	101
Celery juice	33
Legumes	31
Noodle soup	236
Pear compote	100
Pear juice	180
Potato with dandelion salad	162
Radish with horseradish	196
Rice congee with honey pear and black sesame	158
Rice noodle soup with shiitake mushrooms	65
Rice porridge with orange peel	119
Rice porridge with shrubs (seeds) Yi Yi Ren	211
Rice with parsnips	206
Roasted nuts	973
Rosemary Potatoes	188
Tea from lavender blossoms	0
Tea from sage	4
Tea Green tea	2
Tea liver lather	0
Vegetable miso soup with tofu	106
Vegetable semolina soup	198

4 Snack

5 Lunch

6 Dinner

7 Any time

8 Recipes

(recommendable) = You can use more.
(little) = You should use less than specified or omit.

8.1 8 treasures of rice

Strengthens kidney and bladder, builds up Qi, strengthens the spleen, repels moisture, reduces internal heat, prevents cancer, builds heart, calms nerves.
 Cooking time approx. 1 hour
4 portions

Quantity of ingredients
Lily bulbs 1 table spoon / 5g. (recommended)...................................*
Longane 1 table spoon / 5g. (recommended)....................................*
King Solomon's-seal 1 table spoon / 5g. (recommended)..................*
Yam root, yam root tuber 1 table spoon / 5g. (recommended)...........*
Coix (seeds) YiYi Ren 1 table spoon / 5g. (recommended) ....*
Rice wild (nature rice) 1 1/2 cups / 240g. (recommended)..........metal
Water 8-10 cups / 800g. (yes) .... earth

Cooking instructions:
Each one 1 tbsp: Bai He, Longan, Yu Zhu, Da Zao, Shan Yao, Lian Mi, Yi Yi Ren, Qian Shi
Add hot water and soak for about 30 minutes. Then add 1 - 2 cups of rice (normal) and simmer for 1/2 to 1 hour until the rice is very soft. Or: Cook for about 3 hours with the herbs a congee. Then the herbs do not have to be soaked.

8.2 Adzuki Bean and Rice Soup

Reduces moisture, directs down, reduces gastrointestinal heat, builds up essence, strengthens muscles after heat illness, builds up body fluids.
Cooking time approx. 2 hours
Calories p. portion: 199
1 portions

Quantity of ingredients
Adzuki beans 8 table spoons / 40g. (recommended)..................water
Rice round grain 2 table spoons / 20g. (recommended).............metal
Water 1 1/2 cups / 200g. (yes)... earth
Honey 1 table spoon / 8g. (recommended) .... earth

Cooking instructions:
Boil soaked adzuki beans and round grain rice in a ratio of 4: 1 in water until a thin pulp has formed. Sweet as needed; possibly puree.

Effect: This recipe strengthens kidney, spleen and stomach and is particularly suitable for mothers with too little milk flow.

8.3 Barley soup

Works neutral to slightly warming and relaxes the Qi flow. Helps with loss of appetite and diarrhea due to spleen weakness. With weak spleen qi, one should often eat salty soups for breakfast.
Cooking time approx. 25 min
Calories p. portion: 265
2 portions
Allergens: A

Quantity of ingredients
Barley 1 cup / 120g. (recommended).. earth
Salt 1 pinch / 1g. (recommended)...water
Ginger fresh 1/2 teaspoon / 1g. (recommended).......................metal
Olive oil 1 table spoon / 10g. (little).. earth
Parsley 2 table spoons / 30g. (yes)...wood
Water 1 1/2 cups / 240g. (yes).. earth

Cooking instructions:
Roast the barley in the pan, then grind it to the ground, and boil with water, some salt and ginger to a mash. Before serving add oil and parsley.

Variant: You can add a better taste to the dish if you cook it with prepared vegetable or meat broth.

8.4 Barley water

Moisturizes the lungs and large intestine, forces spleen, cools bladder, moisturizes intestines, relaxes, builds up Qi, spreads, forces spleen, passes downwardly.
Cooking time approx. 2 hours
Calories p. portion: 44
10 portions
Allergens: A

Quantity of ingredients
Barley 1/4 lbs - 4oz / 100g. (recommended) .... earth
Water 8 cup - 1/2 1 Gallons / 1900g. (yes)................................ earth
Lemon peel 1 knife tip / 1g. (recommended).............................. fire
Cinnamon ground 1 pinch / 1g. () .... *
Fig 4-5 pieces / 100g. (yes)... earth
Ginger fresh 1 pinch / 1g. (recommended)................................metal
Clove 1 piece / 0,5g. (recommended) ....metal
Salt 1 pinch / 1g. (recommended)..water
Cocoa 1 pinch / 1g. (recommended).. fire

Cooking instructions:
Give the barley in a pot of 2 l. water and let it swell for 5 hours. Then heat the barley, add the fig, cinnamon, clove, ginger and salt. Simmer for 2 hours and strain the hot barley water. Add the grated lemon peel and cocoa.

8.5 Basic recipe for a beef broth (clear)

Strengthens Qi and Yang, is very warming.
Cooking time approx. 4-8 hours
Calories p. portion: 114
10 portions
Allergens: O

Quantity of ingredients
Beef soup meat 1,1 lbs / 500g. .... earth
Beef meatbones 5/8 oz / 200g. .... earth
Vinegar (Red wine vinegar) 1 dash / 3g. ....wood
Juniper berry 8 pieces / 6g. .... fire
Rosemary 1 pinch / 1g. .... fire
Carrot 3 pieces / 210g. .... earth
Parsnip 2 pieces / 300g. .... fire
Leek 1 piece / 200g. ....metal
Ginger fresh 1/2 teaspoon / 5g. ....metal
Lovage 1 stem / 15g. ....metal
Clove 2 pieces / 2g. ....metal
Pimento 6 pieces / 12g. ....metal
Anise (Common Fennel) 2 pieces / 1g. .... earth
Salt 1 teaspoon / 5g. ....water
Water 3,3 lbs / 1300g. .... earth

Cooking instructions:
Heat water, a dash of red wine vinegar, some juniper berries, a little rosemary, bones and meat till it boils; add carrot, parsnip, leek, ginger, lovage, clove, allspice, star anise and a little salt; simmer for 4-8 hours then strain.
Refrigerate for later use.

8.6   Basic recipe for a chicken broth worming

Strengthens Qi and blood, is very warm.
Cooking time approx. 2-3 hours
Calories p. portion: 90
9 portions
Allergens: L

Quantity of ingredients

Chicken meat 1/2 piece / 600g. ....wood
Carrot 2 pieces / 150g. .... earth
Leek 1 stick / 45g. ....metal
Celery root 1 piece / 500g. .... earth
Ginger fresh 2 slices / 2g. ....metal
Fenugreek (Trigonella foenum-graecum) 1 teaspoon / 2g. ....*
Juniper berry 1 teaspoon / 3g. .... fire
Bay leaf 3 pieces / 2g. ....*
Water 4 cup / 900g. .... earth

Cooking instructions:

Remove chicken parts from fat. Place chicken pieces in a saucepan with hot water and heat till it boils briefly, skimming any resulting foam. Add coarsely chopped vegetables and all spices and cook over medium heat for 2 to 3 hours. Strain the finished soup. Throw away vegetables and bones.
Tip: If you want to use the meat as a soup insert, take out after 45 minutes and return only the bones in the soup.
Refrigerate for later use.

8.7   Basic recipe for a duck broth

Forces Qi, strengthens blood and fluids, nourishes Yin, forces stomach, cools heat, strengthens spleen and liver.
Cooking time approx. 2-3 hours
Calories p. portion: 61
6 portions
Allergens: L

Quantity of ingredients

Duck (heart) 5/8 oz / 200g. .... wood
Water 2 cup / 450g. .... earth
Duck (slaughtered) 1/4 lbs - 4oz / 100g. .... wood
Carrot 2 pieces / 100g. .... earth
Celery root 1/2 piece / 600g. .... earth

Cooking instructions:

Cook duck pieces with vegetables for 2-3 hours. Sift broth through a fine sieve and refrigerate for later use.
The innards can be reused: You cut them finely and leaves them for a few minutes with fresh vegetables in the broth draw. Sprinkle with parsley before serving.

8.8   Basic recipe for a fish broth

Strengthens kidney Qi and Yin, strengthens blood and fluids, promotes urination.
Cooking time approx. 40 min
Calories p. portion: 128
5 portions
Allergens: DLO

Quantity of ingredients

Fish pieces mixed (fresh water) 3/4 lbs / 300g. .... water
Celery root 1/4 lbs - 4oz / 120g. .... earth
Leek 2 inches / 10g. .... metal
Carrot 2 pieces / 150g. .... earth
White wine 1/2 cup / 125g. .... wood
Lemon 1/2 piece / 50g. .... wood
Bay leaf 2 leaves / 2g. .... *
Peppercorns 3 pieces / 2g. .... metal
Olive oil 1 table spoon / 10g. .... earth
Water 2 cup / 450g. .... earth

Cooking instructions:

Fry celery, chopped carrots and leeks in olive oil, add bay leaf and peppercorns, add pieces of fish and sauté briefly. Add water, add little white wine or lemon. Simmer gently for 30 minutes. Skim off the resulting foam several times. In the end, sift the ingredients through a cloth. Refrigerate for later use.

8.9 Basic recipe for a reissue soup (Congee)

Warms the stomach and spleen, harmonizes the intestine, forces Qi, reduces moisture.
Cooking time approx. 2-4 hours
Calories p. portion: 140
3 portions
Allergens:

Quantity of ingredients

Rice variety any 1 cup / 120g. ....metal
Water 6 cups / 700g. .... earth

Cooking instructions:

Cook rice and water in a ratio of about 1: 6. The amount of water determines the thickness of the mash (matter of taste).
Put the rice in a saucepan with a heavy lid. It is important to simmer the rice after a short boil on the slightest flame, otherwise it burns.
Boil the rice for 2-4 hours. The longer he cooks, the more he strengthens.
If you want to eat the dish for breakfast, you can put the rice on just before bedtime.
To be on the safe side, you should first check the behavior of your pot and cooker under observation for a similar amount of time, so that nothing burns.
Refrigerate for later use.

8.10 Basic recipe for a vegetable soup, nutritious

Strengthens spleen and lung, regulates Qi flow, builds up Qi, dries out, passes downwardly, strengthens stomach Qi.
Cooking time approx. 2-3 hours
Calories p. portion: 48
5 portions
Allergens: L

Quantity of ingredients

Olive oil 1 table spoon / 4g. .... earth
Onion white 1 piece / 60g. ....metal
Carrot 3 pieces / 200g. .... earth
Parsnip 3/8 lbs - 6oz / 150g. .... fire
Celery root 1 cup / 100g. .... earth
Ginger fresh 1/2 teaspoon / 2g. ....metal

Lemon 1/2 piece / 25g. .... wood
Juniper berry 6 pieces / 6g. .... fire
Thyme dried 1 pinch / 1g. .... metal
Lovage 1 table spoon / 3g. .... metal
Bay leaf 2 leaves / 1g. .... *
Salt 1 pinch / 1g. .... water
Water 3 cups / 650g. .... earth

Cooking instructions:
Cut the vegetables into cubes.
Heat oil in hot pot, fry shortly onions and vegetables.
Add cold water, then add ginger, bay leaf and lemon juice.
Season with juniper, thyme and lovage. Cover for 2 - 3 hours on a low heat and simmer.
The used vegetables should be thrown away.
The basic recipe serves as a soup base and to refine vegetables, legumes or cereals.
If you want to eat vegetable soup immediately, add the desired vegetables half an hour before.
Refrigerate for later use.

8.11 Beluga lentil stew with vegetables

Tonifies Qi and blood, forces kidneys and spleen, dissipates heat and moisture.
Cooking time approx. 20 min
Calories p. portion: 201
5 portions

Quantity of ingredients
Lentils 1 1/2 cups / 240g. (recommended) .... water
Water 4-5 cups / 500g. (yes) .... earth
Carrot 3 pieces / 150g. (recommended).................................... earth
Leek 1 piece / 300g. (recommended) .... metal
Kohlrabi 1/2 piece / 200g. (recommended) .... earth
Tomato 2 pieces / 80g. ()... wood
Onion white 1 piece / 50g. (recommended)............................... metal
Bay leaf 2 leaves / 1g. (recommended) .... *
Fennel 1 piece / 250g. (recommended) .... earth
Star anise 2 pieces / 1g. (little) .... *
Juniper berry 6 pieces / 2g. (yes)... fire

Olive oil 2 table spoons / 30g. (little) .... earth
Salt 1 pinch / 1g. (recommended)..water
Ginger fresh 1/2 teaspoon / 2g. (recommended).......................metal
Black caraway 1 pinch / 1g. (recommended) ....*

Cooking instructions:
Heat oil in hot pot. Fry onions and add diced vegetables and spices, lentils (washed well) and salt. Cover with cold water (3 fingers wide) and cook for 20 minutes on a low heat.
Sprinkle with fresh herbs and black cumin

Goes well with rice!

8.12 Black-eyed beans stew

Strengthens spleen and kidney, is very nutritious, warms the stomach and spleen, harmonizes the intestine, forces Qi, strengthens stomach and kidney, strengthens spleen and kidney.
Cooking time approx. 20 min
Calories p. portion: 140
5 portions

Quantity of ingredients
Black-eyed peas 1 cup / 100g. (yes)..water
Rice variety any 1 1/2 cups / 200g. (recommended) ....metal
Water 10 cups / 1000g. (yes)... earth

Cooking instructions:
Soak the beans overnight and strain.

In a ratio of 1: 2, simmer the beans together with the rice in the Water. Depending on how hot the flame is and how thin the dish should be, more water must be added.

Variation: Add vegetables fried in oil, such as carrots, celery tubers, onions or leeks.

8.13 Carrot and rice gruel soup

Warms the stomach and spleen, harmonizes the intestine, forces Qi, reduces moisture, strengthens spleen and liver, regulates Qi flow, moisturizes, relaxes, builds up Qi, spreads.
Cooking time approx. 10 min
Calories p. portion: 101
1 portions

Quantity of ingredients
Basic recipe for a rice soup (Congee) 1 cup / 120g. (yes) .... *
Carrot 2 pieces / 100g. (recommended) .... earth
Salt 1 teaspoon / 4g. (recommended) .... water

Cooking instructions:
Peel and grate carrots. Heat the rice soup (according to the basic recipe) till it boils and add the grated carrots and salt. Cook for 10 minutes.

8.14 Celery juice

Strengthens stomach Qi, moisturizes, relaxes, builds up Qi, spreads.
Cooking time approx. 5 min
Calories p. portion: 33
1 portions
Allergens: L

Quantity of ingredients
Celery root 1/2 piece / 200g. (recommended) .... earth
Water 1 cup / 120g. (yes) .... earth
Salt 1 pinch / 0,5g. (recommended) .... water

Cooking instructions:
Peel celeriac and cut into pieces and juice. Mix with water and salt as needed.

8.15 Indian Dal soup

Reduces internal heat and moisture, softens, passes downwardly, strengthens spleen and liver, regulates Qi flow, moisturizes, relaxes, builds up Qi, spreads, forces liver and kidney, reduces damp heat.
Cooking time approx. 30 min
Calories p. portion: 256
2 portions
Allergens: EN

Quantity of ingredients
Lentils 3/8 lbs - 6oz / 175g. (recommended) ....water
Sesame oil 2 table spoons / 30g. (little) ....earth
Carrot 1 piece / 100g. (recommended) ....earth
Onion (shallot) 1 piece / 15g. (recommended) ....metal
Water 1 1/2 cups / 200g. (yes)..earth
Ginger fresh 2 slices / 1g. (recommended) ....metal
Salt 1 pinch / 0,5g. (recommended)..water
Soy sauce 1 teaspoon / 3g. (recommended)...............................water
Parsley 1 teaspoon (chopped) / 3g. (yes) ....wood
Thyme 1 teaspoon / 3g. (yes)..*
Basil 1 table spoon / 5g. (yes) ....metal

Cooking instructions:
Soak the lentils overnight.
in a hot pot, carrot, onion and a little ginger fry, pour water. Add the lentils and cook until soft. Add salt or soy sauce and cook for another 10 minutes.
Stir in parsley before serving; Sprinkle thyme or basil over it.
Variant: Other herbs such as sage, rosemary or lovage allow a variety of flavors.

8.16 Legumes

Strengthens spleen and liver, regulates Qi flow, moisturizes, relaxes, builds up Qi, spreads, nourishes blood and Qi, diuretic, harmonizes Qi (in the middle and lower heater), detoxifies, reduces internal heat and moisture.
Cooking time approx. 30 min
Calories p. portion: 31
5 portions

Quantity of ingredients

Pinto beans speckled 1/4 lbs - 4oz / 100g. (recommended) .... water
Lentils 1/8 lbs - 2oz / 50g. (recommended) .... water
Peas, green 1/8 lbs - 2oz / 50g. (recommended) .... water
Water 4 cup / 1000g. (yes) .... earth
Lemon 1 slice / 2g. () .... wood
Juniper berry 6 pieces / 2g. (yes) .... fire
Thyme 1 Twig / 3g. (yes) .... *
Rosemary 1 Twig / 3g. (yes) .... fire
Carrot 1 piece / 100g. (recommended) .... earth
Savory 1-2 teaspoons / 5g. (recommended) .... water
Ginger fresh a great piece / 3g. (recommended) .... metal
Bay leaf 2-3 leaves / 1g. (recommended) .... *
Wakame 1-2 strips / 1g. (recommended) .... water

Cooking instructions:

Legumes such as beans, lentils, peas or chickpeas are soaked in plenty of cold water for several hours to three days. The water should be changed every 8 hours. Then pour off soaking water and wash legumes thoroughly.

Preparation:
Cook the legumes with fresh cold water and a slice of ginger and bring to froth. Cook without lid for about 5 minutes, scooping off the foam. Only then add the following ingredients: a slice of lemon or lemon juice, crush juniper berries, thyme; (possibly 1 knife tip of asafoetida in case of severe indigestion). Add savory, sage, juniper, fenugreek seeds, carrots, bay leaves, fresh ginger, wakame algae.

Simmer on the slightest flame until beans or lentils have the desired consistency.
This base can be stored for 3-4 days in the refrigerator.

8.17 Lentils and rice stew

Strengthens spleen and liver, regulates Qi flow, moisturizes, relaxes, builds up Qi, spreads, warms the stomach and spleen, harmonizes the intestine, forces Qi, reduces moisture, brings the liver Qi in motion, cools heat.
Cooking time approx. 25 min
Calories p. portion: 232
3 portions
Allergens: LNO

Quantity of ingredients

Lentils 1/4 lbs - 4oz / 100g. (recommended) .... water
Water 5 cups / 500g. (yes) .... earth
Rice variety any 1 cup / 120g. (recommended) .... metal
Sesame oil 1 table spoon / 10g. (little) .... earth
Carrot 2 pieces / 150g. (recommended) .... earth
Celery sticks 2 rods / 20g. (recommended) .... earth
Cumin (Caraway seed) 1 pinch / 0,2g. (recommended) .... metal
Salt 1 pinch / 0,5g. (recommended) .... water
Vinegar (Apple vinegar) 1 dash / 2g. (recommended) .... wood
Parsley 2 table spoons / 18g. (yes) .... wood

Cooking instructions:

Soak the dry lentils the day before.
Heat sesame oil in a hot pot; cut carrot and celery into small pieces and sauté; add rice, a pinch of cumin and lentils and heat till it boils.
If the lenses are soft, add salt; season with a little vinegar and garnish with parsley.

Variant: In summer you can omit the cumin and add fresh green peas, Chinese cabbage or celery.

8.18 Noodle soup

Nourishes lung Yin, produces humors, strengthens spleen and liver, regulates Qi flow, moisturizes, relaxes, builds up Qi, spreads, forces Qi and blood, reduces cold, strengthens spleen and stomach, preserves the fluids, contracts.
Cooking time approx. 1 1/2 hours
Calories p. portion: 237
8 portions
Allergens: ACEGL

Quantity of ingredients

Beef soup meat 3/4 lbs / 300g. (recommended) .... earth
Water 4 cup / 900g. (yes) .... earth
Bay leaf 1 piece / 1g. (recommended) .... *
Carrot 3/4 lbs / 300g. (recommended) .... earth
Celery sticks 1 bunch / 200g. (recommended) .... earth
Cauliflower 3/4 lbs / 300g. (recommended) .... earth
Parsley 1 Bunch / 100g. (yes) .... wood
Noodles (wheat) with egg 3/4 lbs / 300g. (recommended) .... wood

Butter organic 1 table spoon / 10g. (little)................................... earth
Salt 1 teaspoon / 2g. (recommended)..water
Soy sauce 1 table spoon / 8g. (recommended).........................water
Tomato paste 1 table spoon / 10g. (recommended)...................wood

Cooking instructions:
Simmer the meat and bay leaf in the water over low heat for about 30 minutes. Peel and slice the carrots. From the celery plant separate the lower end and the leaves. Wash the stems, peel off the tough threads and cut the stems into slices about 1 cm thick.
Wash the Brussels sprouts, clean them and cut the roses from below crosswise.
Wash and chop the parsley.

Add the Brussels sprouts and carrot slices to the soup and cook for about 30 minutes.

After about 10 minutes, add the celery and green leaves and the pasta. Finally, remove the bay leaf and celery green.

(For the baby, remove about 200-250 g of carrots, celery and noodles with broth, squeeze about 35 g of meat finely and add to the baby soup, stir in the butter and 1 teaspoon of chopped parsley.)

Season the remaining soup with the salt, the soy sauce, the tomato paste and the remaining parsley. Lift out the meat. Remove fat and bones and dice the meat. Serve in the soup.

8.19 Pear compote

Moisturizes lungs, reduces lung mucus, nourishes lungs Qi.
Cooking time approx. 20 min
Calories p. portion: 100
3 portions

Quantity of ingredients
Water 1 1/2 cups / 240g. (yes)... earth
Pear 4 / 500g. (recommended)... earth

Cooking instructions:
Halve organic pears. Cores and skin can be used. Pear in the pot and add water. Simmer for up to 20 minutes until pears are tender.

8.20 Pear juice

Moisturizes lungs, reduces lung mucus, nourishes lungs Qi.
Cooking time approx. 5 min
Calories p. portion: 180
2 portions

Quantity of ingredients
Pear 3 pieces / 600g. (recommended)....................................... earth

Cooking instructions:
Peel pears thinly (vitamins under the skin) and core. Juice in the juicer.

8.21 Potato with dandelion salad

Forces Qi, forces spleen, relieves inflammation, moisturizes, relaxes,
builds up Qi, cools liver fire, reduces internal heat, softens knots,
dissolves stagnation, passes downwardly, nourishes fluids und Jing,
builds up Qi, spreads.
Cooking time approx. 25 min
Calories p. portion: 162
2 portions

Quantity of ingredients
Potato 5/8 lbs - 8oz / 250g. (recommended) .... earth
Onion white 1/2 piece / 20g. (recommended)............................metal
Sunflower oil 1 table spoon / 10g. (little) .... earth
Dandelion (young plants) 1/4 lbs - 4oz / 125g. (yes) .... fire
Salt 1 pinch / 1g. (recommended)...water
Pepper white (ground) 1 pinch / 0,5g. (little)..............................metal

Cooking instructions:
Cook the potatoes in salted water and cut into thin slices. Finely chop
the onion. Now season the potatoes with oil, salt and pepper and add
the dandelion and mix.

8.22 Radish with horseradish

Slightly refreshing and moisturizing, dissolves stagnation, nourishes blood and liver, harmonizes liver and spleen, forces eyesight, preserves the fluids, contracts, nourishes the lungs and spleen, distributes mucus, dissolves mucus, dissolves stagnation, directs upwards.
Cooking time approx. 30 min
Calories p. portion: 196
2 portions
Allergens: GNO

Quantity of ingredients
Butter organic 1 table spoon / 8g. (little)..................................... earth
Radish (white, green, purple-red) 1/2 piece / 50g. (yes)..............metal
Water 2 table spoons / 10g. (yes)... earth
Lemon juice 2 table spoons / 20g. ()..wood
White wine 2 table spoons / 20g. (recommended) ....wood
Pepper powder (hot) 1 pinch / 0,2g. (recommended) .... fire
Sesame oil 1 teaspoon / 3g. (little)... earth
Radish horseradish 2 table spoons / 20g. (yes) ....metal
Salt 1 pinch / 0,5g. (recommended)...water
Parsley 1 Bunch (chopped) / 80g. (yes)....................................wood
Rice long grain rice 1/2 cup / 60g. (recommended)...................metal
Water 3 cups / 300g. (yes) .... earth
Salt 1 pinch / 0,5g. (recommended)...water

Cooking instructions:
In a hot pan melt the butter, sautéed into stripes cut radish. Add cold water, lemon juice, white wine, a pinch of rose paprika and stir in the sesame oil; with 2 - 3 tablespoons fresh grated horseradish (alternatively 1 teaspoon from the glass), salt to taste; Sprinkle with chopped parsley.

Place the rice with the water, salt and cook for about 15 minutes.

8.23 Rice congee with honey pear and black sesame

Especially good in kidney Yin deficiency, moisturizes lungs, cools heat, reduces lung mucus, produces humors, moisturizes, relaxes, builds up Qi, spreads, moisturizes intestines, nourishes Yin.
Cooking time approx. 10 min - 3 hours
Calories p. portion: 158
2 portions
Allergens: N

Quantity of ingredients

Basic recipe for a rice soup (Congee) 1 1/2 cups / 240g. (yes)..........*
Pear 2 pieces / 300g. (recommended)....................................... earth
Sesame, black 1 teaspoon / 3g. (recommended)....................... wood

Cooking instructions:

Cook rice congee according to basic recipe.
Fill pot with 3 cm of water and heat till it boils. Quarter the pears (with the skin and seeds) and simmer them covered with black sesame for 10 minutes. Mix with the rice.

8.24 Rice noodle soup with shiitake mushrooms

Strengthens spleen and liver, regulates Qi flow, relaxes, builds up Qi, spreads, dries out, passes downwardly, strengthens stomach Qi, nourishes Yin of the lungs, stomach and colon, supports digestion, reduces internal wind.
Cooking time approx. 20 min
Calories p. portion: 66
2 portions
Allergens: L

Quantity of ingredients

Rice noodles 2 handful / 20g. (recommended)...........................metal
Shiitake, dried 4-6 pieces / 5g. (recommended)......................... earth
Basic recipe for a vegetable soup (nutritious) 1 1/2 cups / 240g. (recommended)*
Chinese cabbage 1 cup / 60g. (recommended)......................... earth
Lovage 1 teaspoon / 3g. (recommended) ....metal
Miso 2 table spoons / 18g. (yes)..water

Cooking instructions:

Soak rice noodles and shiitake mushrooms separately in cold water. Heat the vegetable broth and add the soaked shiitake mushrooms cut into strips and simmer gently. Cut Chinese cabbage into noodles, add lovage green and rice noodles and let it steep for a while. Before serving, stir in Miso dissolved in a little cooled water. Recommendation: Suitable at the beginning of each meal, also for breakfast.

8.25 Rice porridge with orange peel

Warms the stomach and spleen, harmonizes the intestine, forces Qi, reduces moisture. brings the Liver Qi in motion, cools heat, moisturizes, relaxes, builds up Qi, spreads. nourishes blood, moisturizes, relaxes, builds up Qi, spreads.
Cooking time approx. 10 min
Calories p. portion: 120
4 portions
Allergens: L

Quantity of ingredients
Rice variety any 1 cup / 100g. (recommended)..........................metal
Water 6 cups / 600g. (yes) .... earth
Orange grated peel 1/4 piece / 3g. (recommended)..........................*
Olive oil 1 table spoon / 10g. (little).. earth
Champignon 1/2 cup / 50g. (recommended)............................. earth
Celery sticks 1/2 bunch / 60g. (recommended)........................... earth
Basic recipe for a chicken soup 3-4 table spoons / 40g. (yes)...........*
Salt 1 pinch / 0,5g. (recommended)...water

Cooking instructions:
The day before boil the rice with the orange peel and water in a ratio of about 1: 6. The amount of water determines the thickness of the mash (pure matter of taste). Put the rice in a saucepan with good insulation and a heavy lid. It is important to simmer the rice after a short boil on the slightest flame, otherwise it burns. Boil the rice for 2-4 hours. The longer he cooks, the more he strengthens.
Heat the oil in a saucepan, add the chopped champignon and celery and sauté briefly. Add the rice. Add vegetable broth or water, warm up, salt.

8.26 Rice porridge with shrubs (seeds) Yi Yi Ren

Warms stomach, harmonizes the intestine, forces Qi, reduces moisture, forces spleen, nourishes and forces Lunge, reduces internal heat, moves Qi and blood, diuretic, cools in internal heat.
Cooking time approx. 25 min
Calories p. portion: 212
2 portions

Quantity of ingredients

Water 4 cups / 450g. (yes) .... earth
Rice variety any 1 cup / 120g. (recommended) .... metal
Lemon peel 1/4 piece / 2g. (recommended) .... fire
Coix (seeds) YiYi Ren 1/2 cup / 50g. (recommended) .... *
Cress 1 table spoon / 6g. (recommended) .... metal

Cooking instructions:
Cook rice porridge according to basic recipe with a half cup of Yi Yi Ren and lemon peel. Simmer for 1 hour and then sprinkle cress over it.

8.27 Rice soup with grated carrots and fresh herbs

Strengthens spleen and liver, regulates Qi flow, moisturizes, relaxes, builds up Qi, spreads, forces kidney and bladder.
Cooking time approx. 5 min
Calories p. portion: 131
4 portions
Allergens: EG

Quantity of ingredients

Rice wild (nature rice) 1 cup / 100g. (recommended) .... metal
Water 6 cups / 700g. (yes) .... earth
Carrot 1 piece / 100g. (recommended) .... earth
Soy sauce 1 dash / 2g. (recommended) .... water
Butter organic 1 teaspoon / 3g. (little) .... earth
Ground 1 pinch / 0,3g. (recommended) .... earth
Curcuma 1 pinch / 0,2g. (yes) .... *
Herbs various 1 teaspoon (chopped) / 3g. (recommended) .... *

Cooking instructions:
In a portion of rice congee according to basic recipe, softly cook a grated carrot, add butter and soy sauce.
Sprinkle with fresh herbs.

Spices and herbs: black cumin, turmeric, cardamom, parsley, sage, thyme, basil, rosemary.

Winter: parsnip, celery, onion, leek, pumpkin
Summer: tomatoes, zucchini, spring onion, radishes, arugula.

8.28 Rice with parsnips

Regulates Qi, dries out, passes downwardly, warms the stomach and spleen, harmonizes the intestine, forces Qi, reduces moisture. moisturizes, relaxes, builds up Qi, spreads. distributes mucus, activates Wei Qi, forces Qi.
Cooking time approx. 45 min
Calories p. portion: 206
3 portions

Quantity of ingredients
Rice variety any 1 cup / 120g. (recommended)..........................metal
Water 1 1/2 cups / 200g. (yes)... earth
Salt 1 pinch / 1g. (recommended)..water
Parsnip 3-4 pieces / 450g. (recommended) .... fire
Olive oil 1 table spoon / 10g. (little)... earth
Sage 1 teaspoon / 3g. (recommended).. fire

Cooking instructions:
Peel the parsnips and cut into slices. Fry for a short time in oil. Add the rice and fry again for a short time. Add the water and cook it at least 30 min. Sprinkle with fresh chopped sage.

8.29 Rice with stewed vegetables

Dissipates heat and moisture.
Cooking time approx. 20 min
Calories p. portion: 166
2 portions
Allergens: L

Quantity of ingredients
Rice variety any 1/2 cup / 60g. (recommended) ....metal
Water 3 cups / 300g. (yes) .... earth
Lemon peel 1 piece / 3g. (recommended)..................................... fire
Water 1/2 cup / 0g. (yes)... earth
Carrot 2 pieces / 180g. (recommended).................................... earth
Celery sticks 1/2 piece / 5g. (recommended) .... earth
Champignon 1/2 cup / 50g. (recommended)............................... earth
Cress 2 table spoons / 20g. (recommended) ....metal
Linseed oil 1 dash / 3g. (recommended)................................... earth

Cooking instructions:
Cook rice according to basic recipe with a piece of lemon peel.
Steam chopped carrots, celery and mushrooms until soft.
Then sprinkle with cress. Then add a dash of high quality cold oil.

8.30 Roasted nuts

Strengthens kidney Qi, essence and brain, forces kidney, builds up essence, warms lungs, moistens the intestine, moisturizes, relaxes, builds up Qi, spreads.
Cooking time approx. 5 min
Calories p. portion: 973
2 portions
Allergens: H

Quantity of ingredients
Hazelnuts 1/4 lbs - 4oz / 100g. (recommended)........................ earth
Cashews 1/4 lbs - 4oz / 100g. (recommended)......................... earth
Walnuts 1/4 lbs - 4oz / 100g. (recommended)........................... earth

Cooking instructions:
Roast nuts in a pan for about 5 minutes.

8.31 Rosemary Potatoes

Forces Qi, forces spleen, relieves inflammation, relaxes, builds up Qi, spreads.
Cooking time approx. 30 min
Calories p. portion: 188
2 portions

Quantity of ingredients
Potato 6-8 pieces / 420g. (recommended) .... earth
Salt (herbal) 1 pinch / 1g. (recommended)...............................water
Olive oil 1 table spoon / 10g. (little)... earth
Rosemary 1 teaspoon / 2g. (yes).. fire

Cooking instructions:
Cut the potatoes into half´s, apply a little olive oil on the cut surface, then salt, sprinkle 2 - 3 rosemary needles on the potatoes.
Place the potatoes on the baking tray and bake them in the preheated oven for approx. 25 minutes to 190°C/374°F.

8.32 Tea from celery sticks

Brings the Liver Qi in motion, cools heat, moisturizes, relaxes, builds up Qi, spreads.
Cooking time approx. 15 min
Calories p. portion: 1
4 portions
Allergens: L

Quantity of ingredients
Celery sticks 2 table spoons (chopped) / 18g. (recommended) .. earth
Water 2 cup / 500g. (yes) .... earth

Cooking instructions:
Heat the water till it boils and put it aside. Add cutted celery and cook for 10 min. to let go. Strain. Sweet to taste with honey.

8.33 Tea from ground

Reduces mucus and moist heat in the liver and gallbladder, against liver Qi stagnation, spleen qi deficiency, spleen and kidney Yang-Mangel.
Cooking time approx. 10 min
Calories p. portion: 2
4 portions

Quantity of ingredients
Ground 1 teaspoon / 3g. (recommended) .... earth
Water 2 cup / 500g. (yes) .... earth

Cooking instructions:
Heat the water till it boils and put it aside. Add crushed cumin and leave for 10 min. to let go. Sweet to taste with honey. Strain when pouring.

Drink 1 cup 2 times a day.

8.34 Tea from lavender blossoms

Cooking time approx. 10 min
Calories p. portion: 0
1 portions

Quantity of ingredients
Lavender blossoms 1 teaspoon / 2g. (recommended)......................*
Water 1 cup / 125g. (yes)... earth

Cooking instructions:
Heat the water till it boils and put it aside. Add lavender flowers and 10 min. to let go. Sweet to taste with honey. Strain when pouring.

8.35 Tea from Maidis stigma

Reduces damp heat in the spleen, bladder, liver and bile.
Cooking time approx. 10 min
Calories p. portion: 0
4 portions

Quantity of ingredients
Corn silk tea 1 oz / 30g. (recommended) ....*
Water 2 cup / 500g. (yes)... earth

Cooking instructions:
Heat the water till it boils. Add corn silk and simmer 5 min. Sweet to taste with honey. Strain when pouring.

8.36 Tea from sage

Distributes mucus, passes downwardly, activates Wei Qi, forces Qi.
Cooking time approx. 15 min
Calories p. portion: 4
4 portions

Quantity of ingredients
Sage 2 teaspoons / 6g. (recommended)....................................... fire
Water 2 cup / 500g. (yes)... earth

Cooking instructions:
Heat the water till it boils and put it aside. Add sage and 10 min. to let go. Strain. Sweet to taste with honey.

8.37 Tea from savory

Tonifies the kidney-Yang, the stomach and spleen Qi and warms the middle, forces the liver Qi and the blood, conducts mucus and cold from the lungs, opens the surface, derives wind-cold.
Cooking time approx. 10 min
Calories p. portion: 1
4 portions

Quantity of ingredients
Savory 2-4 teaspoons / 9g. (recommended) ....water
Water 2 cup / 500g. (yes).. earth

Cooking instructions:
Brew dried savory with boiling water and cover for about 10 minutes. Strain the tea and drink warm.

8.38 Tea from yarrow

Dries out, passes downwardly.
Cooking time approx. 15 min
Calories p. portion: 0
2 portions

Quantity of ingredients
Yarrow tea 2-4 teaspoons / 6g. (recommended) .... fire
Water 2 cup / 500g. (yes).. earth

Cooking instructions:
Heat the water till it boils and put it aside. Add yarrow and 10 min. to let go. Strain. Sweet to taste with honey.

8.39 Tea Green tea

Reduces internal heat, dissolves mucus, detoxifies.
Cooking time approx. 10 min
Calories p. portion: 2
1 portions

Quantity of ingredients
Green tea 1 teaspoon / 2g. (recommended) .... fire
Water 1 cup / 120g. (yes) .... earth

Cooking instructions:
For each cup you use a teaspoonful or a teabag.
Pour green tea only with 60 to 80 ° C / 140 to 176 °F hot water, otherwise it will be bitter.
If the tea has a stimulating effect, let it draw for two to three minutes. It has a calming effect for a duration of five minutes (no longer, otherwise it will be bitter!).
Another method: Pour the tea leaves with about 70 ° C / 158 °F hot water and pour the water immediately again. Then just pour hot water again. The bitter substances disappear and the tea gets a milder aroma.

8.40 Tea liver lather

Reduces moist heat in the liver and gallbladder.
Cooking time approx. 10 min
Calories p. portion: 0
2 portions

Quantity of ingredients
Liver smoothing tea 2 teaspoons / 4g. (recommended).....................*
Water 2 cup / 500g. (yes) .... earth

Cooking instructions:
Heat the water till it boils and put it aside. Add 2 teaspoons of the tea mixture and stir for 10 min. to let go. Sweet to taste with honey. Strain when pouring.
1/2 cup before and 1/2 cup after eating

8.41 Vegetable miso soup with tofu

Strengthens spleen and liver, regulates Qi flow, moisturizes, relaxes, builds up Qi, spreads, forces Qi, forces liver and kidney, reduces damp heat, detoxifies, nourishes fluids, reduces internal heat, dries out, passes downwardly.
Cooking time approx. 15 min
Calories p. portion: 107
4 portions
Allergens: EN

Quantity of ingredients
Sesame oil 2 table spoons / 35g. (little) .... earth
Onion (shallot) 1 piece / 20g. (recommended) ....metal
Carrot 1 piece / 70g. (recommended) .... earth
Leek 2 inches / 10g. (recommended)..metal
Water 3 cups / 750g. (yes) .... earth
Endive salad 2 table spoons / 30g. (recommended)...................... fire
Soy Tofu 2 table spoons / 30g. (recommended)......................... earth
Ginger fresh 1/2 teaspoon / 1g. (recommended)........................metal
Miso 2 table spoons / 15g. (yes)..water

Cooking instructions:
In sesame oil first sauté onions, then carrots and a little leek; Pour in water and simmer gently; add the bean sprouts and endive leaves and leave to stand; Tofu cubes, add a little ginger; at the end stir in a little cooled cooking-water the Miso.

8.42 Vegetable semolina soup

Strengthens spleen and liver, regulates Qi flow, builds up Qi, dries out, passes downwardly, reduces moisture, regulates Qi.
Cooking time approx. 20 min
Calories p. portion: 199
3 portions
Allergens: AEGL

Quantity of ingredients
Basic recipe for a vegetable soup 2 cup / 500g. (recommended) ....*
Potato 1 piece / 80g. (recommended).. earth
Parsnip 1 piece / 180g. (recommended) .... fire
Carrot 1 piece / 120g. (recommended) .... earth
Celery root 3/8 lbs - 6oz / 150g. (recommended) .... earth
Kohlrabi 1/2 piece / 200g. (recommended) .... earth

Beans (green, fresh) 1/4 lbs / 100g. (recommended) ....water
Wheat semolina 2 table spoons / 24g. (recommended).............. wood
Lovage 1/2 teaspoon / 2g. (recommended) ....metal
Butter organic 1 table spoon / 20g. (little)................................ earth
Soy sauce 1 teaspoon / 3g. (recommended)............................water

Cooking instructions:

Worm the prepared vegetable soup; cook the vegetables in the soup softly. Spread some wheatgrass and let it swell. At the end, add lovage-green and a little butter and taste with soy sauce.

9 Effects of food

9.1 Use ingredients: recommendable

Acai powder
Acerola fruit nectar or powder
Adzuki beans
Agar agar (kelp)
Agave nectar
Agrimony
Almond marzipan
Almond milk
Almond puree
Aloe juice
Amaranth Pops
Angelica root
Anise (Common Fennel)
Apple (sweet)
Apple puree
Apricot
Apricot dried
Apricot jam
Apricot nectar
Apricots juice
Arrowroot
Artichoke
Baking powder
Balm
Bamboo shoots
Banchatee (green tea)
barberry
Barley
Barley flour
Barley grass powder
Barley grouts
Barley malt
Barley not peeled
Basic recipe for a beef soup

Basic recipe for a beef soup (warming)
Basic recipe for a fish soup
Basic recipe for a vegetable soup (nutritious)
Batavia
Bay leaf
Bean oil
Beans (green, fresh)
Bearberry leaf
Beef bone marrow
Beef heart
Beef heart (calf)
Beef kidney
Beef lungs (calf)
Beef Oxtail pieces
Beef soup meat
Beer (alcohol-free)
Beer (alcohol-reduced)
Berries of the season
Berry juice
Bitter Herb liqueur
Bitter Lemon
Bitter liqueur
Bitter orange peel
Black beans
Black caraway
Black fungus mushroom
Blackberry dried (unripe fruit)
Blackberry jam
Blackberry leaves
Blackthorn (Sloe)
Blue mallow tee
Blueberry dried
Blueberry jam

Blueberry juice
Bocksdorn fruits (Fructus Lycii, Goji, goji berry dried
Boletus mushroom
Borage
Borage oil
Brazil nuts
Bread roll
Bread with carob kernel flour
Breadcrumbs (wheat bread, bread roll)
Brie cheese
Broad beans (thick beans)
Broccoli
Brown ale
Brussels sprouts
Buckbean
Buckwheat
Buckwheat (roasted) Kasha
Buckwheat whole grain
Burdock root tea
Bush beans
Butter (half fat)
Butter beans white
Buttermilk
Calamari
Camembert
Campari
Capers in olive oil
Cardamom
Carob flour, St. john's bread
Carrot
Carrot (Early Carrot)
Carrot juice without sugar
Cashews
Cauliflower
Caviar
Celery root
Celery sticks
Chamomile
Chamomile tea
Champignon
Channa-Dal
Chanterelle
Chenpi (chinese tangerine bowl)
Cherry (sour)
Cherry compote
Chervil
Chervil dried
Chestnut puree
Chestnuts
Chicken Blood
Chicken egg white
Chicken heart
Chicken stomach

Chickpeas
Chickweed
Chicory
Chinese cabbage
Chinese pearl barley
Chives
Chlorella (fresh water)
Chocolate (Diabetic)
Chrysanthemum blossom tea
Clarified butter
Clementine
Clementines
Clove
Cocoa
Coconut fat
Coconut meat
Coconut milk
Codfish
Coix (seeds) YiYi Ren
Cola drink
Cola drink (low calorie)
Compote (fruits of the season)
Cooking oil
Coriander
Coriander (fresh)
Corn (fast polenta)
Corn (roasted)
Corn flour
Corn germ oil
Corn Grease (Polenta)
Corn silk tea
Corn starch
Cottage cheese
Crab
Cranberries
Cranberry
Cranberry
Cranberry jam
Cranberry juice
Cream (30% fat)
Cream 10% coffee cream
Cream sour 10%
Cream sour 20%
Cream sour 30%
Cream, sweet 30%
Creamer
Cress
Crispbread
Cucumber (bitter)
Cucumber (spicy cucumber)
Cumin (Caraway seed)
Curd cheese 20%
Curd cheese 40%
Currant jam (black)

Currant jam (red)
Currant juice (black)
Currants (black)
Currants (red)
Curry paste red
Daisy
Dandelion juice
Dandelionroots tea
Dashi
Dates dried
Dates red
Deer meat
Deer's Bones
Deer's kidneys
Dill
Ducks egg
Dulse (seaweed)
Dyer's broom herb
Edam cheese
Eel smoked
Elderberries
Emmental cheese
Endive salad
Evening primrose oil
Fennel
Fennel seeds ground
Fennel tea
Fenugreek (Trigonella foenum-graecum)
Fernet Branca (herbal bitter liqueur)
Feta cheese
Feta cheese
Fish innards
Fish remains
Fish sauce
Flounder
Flower pollen
Fox nut, gorgon nut, makhana
French beans
Fresh cheese
Fresh cheese from soya
Fresh cheese with herbs
Freshwater crab
Fructose (glucose)
Fruit mix juice
Fruit tea
Gail plum
Galangal
Garam Masala powder
Gelatin white
Gelee Royal
Gentian root
Gentian root tea
Ginger fresh

Ginger oil
Ginkgo fruit
Ginseng
Ginseng liqueur
Ginseng root
Goat
Goat and sheep's blood
Goat and sheep's brain
Goat and sheep's liver
Goat and sheep's milk
Goat and sheep's stomach
Goose blood
Goose egg
Goose fat
Gorgonzola
Gouda cheese
Grapefruit dried peel
Grapeseed oil
Green tea
Greengage
Ground
Ground caraway
Guava
Halibut (Flatfish)
Hawthorn
Hazelnuts
Herbal tea mix
Herbs bitter
Herbs of Provence
Herbs various
Herbs wild
Herring
Hibiscus
Hibiscus tea
Hijiki
Hokkaido pumpkin
Honey
Honey wine (Met)
Hop
Horehound leaves
Horse meat
Iceberg lettuce
Jasmine blossoms tee
Jellyfish
Kaki plum
Kalmus
Kefir
Kidney beans (red)
King Solomon's-seal
Kohlrabi
Kombu seaweed (Saccharina japonica)
Kudzu
Kukicha tea
Ladyfingers

Lamb kidneys
Lamb liver
Lamb's lettuce
Lavender blossoms
Leaf salads (bitter)
Leek
Lemon Balm (dried)
Lemon Balm (fresh)
Lemon peel
Lemongrass
Lentils
Lentils black
Lentils red
Lentils yellow
Lettuce
Licorice root tea
Lily bulbs
Lima beans
Lime blossom tea
Linseed
Linseed (crushed)
Linseed oil
Liver smoothing tea
Longane
Loquate / Japanese medlar
Lotus roots
Lotus seeds
Lovage
Lovage seeds
Luo Han Guo fruit
Lychee
Lychee in Preserved
Lychee liqueur
Lye roll
Mackerel
Mallow (Malva sylvestris) blossom tea
Malt
Mango juice
Manioc flour
Maple syrup
Mare's milk
Marjoram
Martini
Mascarpone cheese
Mayonnaise 50%
Mayonnaise 80%
Medlar
Mineral water
Mirabelle plum
Miso black (fermented)
Miso paste (soy bean paste)
Mixed Pickles
Morel, dried
Mu Erh Mushroom

Muesli
Mulberry fruit
Mulled Wine Spice
Multi-grain bread (gray bread)
Mussels
Mustard
Mustard Dijon
Mustard medium hot
Mustard sweet
Mutton
Nasturtium (nose-twister or nose-tweaker)
Nectarine
Nettles
Noodles (wheat) with egg
Noodles (wheat, lasagne) with egg
Noodles (wheat, ribbon noodles) with egg
Noodles (wheat, spaghetti) with egg
Noodles (whole grain) with egg
Nori, purple seaweed, red algae
Oat
Oat flakes (whole grain)
Oat flakes roasted
Oat flour
Oat fusion (baby food)
Oat meal
Oat milk
Octopus
Okra
Olives
Olives green
Onion (shallot)
Onion (spring onion)
Onion read
Onion white
Orange blossom
Orange dried peel
Orange grated peel
Orange jam
Orange peel
Oregano fresh
Oyster mushroom
Oyster shell powder
Palm oil
Parsley root
Parsnip
Passion blossoms tea
Passion fruit
Peaches
Peaches (canned)
Peanut (roasted)
Peanut butter
Peanuts

Pear
Pearl barley
Pearl barley
Peas
Peas, green
Pepper powder (hot)
Peppermint
Peppermint tea
Pepperoni
Pepperoni, red, pitted, halved
Pepperoni, yellow, pitted, halved
Peppers
Peppers powder
Pheasant
Pickle
Pig blood
Pigeon
Pigeon egg
Pinto beans speckled
Plum dried
Plums
Pomegranate
Poppy
Pork Bacon
Pork brain
Pork fat (lard)
Pork ham
Pork ham cooked
Pork ham smoked
Pork heart
Pork kidneys
Pork knuckle
Pork Lard
Pork lung
Pork marrow bones
Pork sausage (Bratwurst) Pork skin
Pork stomach
Pork/beef sausage (smoked)
Pork's intestine
Potato
Potato (mealy)
Potato flour
Prickly pear
Processed cheese 12%
processed cheese 30%
Prosecco
Psyllium seed
Pudding powder vanilla
Puff pastry
Pumpernickel (dark bread)
Pumpkin
Pumpkin seed oil
Quail
Quail egg

Rabbit
Rabbit (wild)
Radicchio
Radish leaves
Raisins
Raspberry dried (immature)
Raspberry jam
Raspberry leaf tea
Red beet
Red berry (without sugar)
Red cabbage
Reishi mushroom
Ribworttea
Rice (fragrance)
Rice (Gaoliang / Sorghum)
Rice (whole grain)
Rice Basmati
Rice black
Rice flour
Rice long grain rice
Rice malt
Rice mash
Rice noodles
Rice red
Rice round grain
Rice starch
Rice sticky
Rice sweet
Rice variety any
Rice wild (nature rice)
Romaine lettuce / lettuce salad
Rose blossom tea
Rose leaf tea
Rosefish
Rum
Rusk
Rye wholemeal bread
Safflower (Dyer's thistle / Hong Hua)
Saffron
Sage
Sago (cereals)
Sake
Salsify
Salt
Salt (herbal)
Savory
Savoy cabbage / kale
Sea buckthorn
Sea cucumber
Sesame oil roasted
Sesame paste (Tahini)
Sesame, black
Sesame, white
Sheep's milk

Sheep's milk yoghurt
Sherry (whine)
Shiitake, dried
Shrimp
Shrimps
Skim milk powder
Slug
Sour cherries
Sour cream 15% fat
Sour milk
Sour milk cheese 20%
Sourdough
Soy flour
Soy noodles
Soy sauce
Soy Tofu
Soy Tofu smoked
Soya Cuisine (soy cream)
Soybean milk
Soybean oil
Soybeans
Soybeans, black
Soybeans, blacks, fermented
Soybeans, yellow
Spelled flakes
Spiny lobsters
Spirit
Spurdog (spiny dogfish, Schillerlocken)
St. Benedict's thistle, blessed thistle,
holy thistle, spotted thistle
Stevia (candyleaf, sweetleaf)
Strawberry jam
Sugar - icing sugar
Sugar palm sugar
Sugar substitute (sweetener)
Sunflower seeds
Supplementary nutrition
Tabasco
Tarragon (Estragon)
Tea mixture uric acid lowering
Thistle oil
Thyme dried
Toast bread (whole grain)
Tomato dried
Tomato juice
Tomato paste
Tomato puree
Tonic Water
Trout (smoked)
Truffle
Tsampa (roasted barley flour)
Turkey ham
Turmeric (yellow root)

Turnip
Turnips
Umeboshi paste
Valerian
Vanilla pod
Vanilla sugar natural
Vegetable juice
Vinegar (Apple vinegar)
Vinegar (Red wine vinegar)
Vinegar Aceto Balsamico
Vinegar Aceto Balsamico white
Wakame
Walnut oil
Walnuts
Wax gourd
Wheat
Wheat flakes
Wheat flatbread/pita bread
Wheat flour whole grain
Wheat semolina
Wheat semolina for children
Wheat/Rye/Gray-black bread with yeast
Wheatgrass juice
Wheatgrass powder
Whey
White beans
White bread (baguette)
White bread (pretzel sticks)
White bread (roll)
White bread (wheat bread)
White breadcrumbs
White cabbage
White dumpling bread (wheat bread cut
into chunks)
White wine
Whitefish
Whole grain bread
Wholemeal flour
Wild boar meat
Wild garlic (garlic spinach)
Wild herbs
Wild strawberries
Wormwood
Wormwood herb
Yam root, yam root tuber
Yarrow
Yarrow tea
Yeast
Yew nut
Yoghurt vanilla
Zucchini

9.2 Use ingredients: yes

Almond
Amaranth
Asparagus (green or white)
Aubergine
Basic recipe for a chicken soup (warming)
Basic recipe for a duck soup
Basic recipe for a rice soup (Congee)
Basil
Basil (fresh)
Black-eyed peas
Chard
Corn
Curcuma
Dandelion (young plants)
Elderberry blossom tee
Fig
Fig dried
Grape juice red
Grape juice white
Grapefruit (Pomelo)
Grapefruit juice
Grapes red
Grapes white
Hyssop
Juniper berry
Lamb's lettuce
Miso
Morel (black, dried)
Octopus
Oregano dried
Oysters
Parsley
Peppers (rose peppers)
Peppers (sweet)
Pine nuts
Pistachios
Pumpkin seeds
Quince
Quinoa
Radish
Radish (white, green, purple-red)
Radish black
Radish horseradish
Rosemary
Rucola
Rye
Rye flour
Seacrab
Spinach
Sugar molasses
Thyme
Vanilla
Vanilla powder
Water
Water hot

9.3 Use ingredients: little

Apple juice (natural cloudy)
Apricots
Avocado
Beef fillet
Beef liver
Beef meat
Beef meat (calf)
Beef meatbones
Beef stomach
Beer (Pils)
Beer (Top-fermented German dark beer)
Blueberry
Boxhorn clover seeds
Bulgur (cereals)
Butter organic
Carp
Cereal coffee
Cherry
Cherry juice
Chicken egg
Chicken liver
Chicken meat
Chicken yolk
Coconut flakes
Coconut grated
Couscous
Cucumber
Duck (heart)
Duck (slaughtered)
Fish pieces mixed (fresh water)
Freshwater fish
Goose
Goose parts
Gourd
Grass carp
Green spelt
Kumquats

Margarine
Margarine (diet)
Millet
Millet flakes
Mustard seeds
Olive oil
Orange juice
Peanut oil
Pear juice
Pepper white (ground)
Perch
Plum
Pork liver
Pork meat
Rabbit liver
Rabbit meat
Rapeseed oil
Raspberry
Rose hip tea
Salmon
Sauerkraut (cutted cabbage fermented)
Sesame oil
Shark
Spelled (Dark) bread
Spelled grain
Spelled semolina
Spelled wholemeal flour
Star anise
Strawberries
Strawberry Juice
Sugar brown
Sugar cane sugar
Sugar fructose - fruit sugar
Sugar glucose - grapes sugar
Sugar Milk Sugar
Sunflower oil
Sweet potato
Tangerine
Topinambur
Trout
Turkey breast meat
Umeboshi plums (Japanese apricots)
Walnuts roasted
Wheat bulgur
Wheat flour
Wheat germ oil

9.4 Do not use contra-acting foods

Anchovy / Sardine
Apple (sour)
Banana
Banana (cooking banana)
Black tea
Blackberry´s
Cantaloupe
Carambola (Star fruit)
Chili (pod or ground)
Chocolate
Cinnamon ground
Cinnamon sticks
Cod
Coffee
Cow's milk (1.5% fat)
Cow's milk (whole milk 3.5% fat)
Créme fraiche cheese
Crucian
Currant (black)
Currant (red)
Currant (white)
Curry
Deer meat
Eel
Garlic
Ginger powder
Goat cheese
Gooseberry
Kiwi
Lamb bones
Lamb meat
Lamb shoulder
Lemon
Lemon juice
Lime
Lobster
Mango
Mediterranean fish (cod, plaice,
haddock, sea Mold cheese
Mozzarella
Mullet
Mung bean
Mung bean sprouting
Mutton
Nutmeg
Orange
Papaya
Parmesan
Pepper (ground)
Pepper Cayenne
Peppercorns
Pimento
Pineapple
Pineapple (from a can)
Pineapple juice without sugar
Plaice

Red wine
Rhubarb
Rose hip
Sorrel
Sugar candy white
Sugar white
Tomato

Tuna
Watermelon
Wheat beer
Wheat bran
Yogi tea
Yogurt (natural, 1.5% fat)
Yogurt (natural, 3.5% fat)

10 Herbs and their effects

10.1 Basil

thermal effect: warm
taste: spicy, bitter
Dries out, leads down. Tonifies Yang and Qi, dissolves mucus-cold, eliminates wind-cold.
It has a beneficial effect on flatulence and nausea, relaxing and soothing. Good to fight emphysema, bronchitis, whooping cough, high blood pressure, headache, mouth odor, warts, hiccup, gout, migraine.

10.2 Savory

thermal effect: warm
taste: bitter
Tonifies kidney yang, heart qi, stomach and spleen qi and warms the middle, moves the liver qi and blood, releases mucous and cold from the lungs, opens the surface, induces wind-cold.
Stomach-strengthening, soothing and appetizing. Ideal for prevent colds, strengthens the immune system. In case of incontinence or nocturnal wetting (not for children), put the beans in liquor for libido.

10.3 Coriander

thermal effect: warm
taste: spicy
Driving sweat, reducing wind, draining moisture, tonifying and regulating qi, eliminating wind-cold.
The essential oils are appetizing, digestive, cramping and soothing in stomach and intestinal disorders.

10.4 Herbs various

Stimulates appetite. Effect different.
Appetizing, lots of trace elements and vitamins.

10.5 Cress

thermal effect: cool
taste: sweet
Moves and tonifies qi and blood, diuretic, cools in internal heat, moisturizes lungs, triggers stagnation, heads upwards.
Diuretic, supports urination. Good to fight dry mouth, inner agitation, sore throat, diabetes, kidney stones, gastrointestinal complaints, lung problems, menstrual cramps or cancer.

10.6 Chives

thermal effect: warm
taste: spicy
Directs upward. Tonifies blood, kidney Yang and Qi. Dissolves moisture. Bactericide, prevents cancer, strengthens gastric juice production, promotes digestion and blood circulation, promotes growth, triggers stagnation.

10.7 Lavender blossoms

thermal effect: warm
taste: spicy, bitter
Do not use during pregnancy. Suppresses internal wind, dissipates moisture and heat. Regulates and moves Qi, tones Qi, moves blood, eliminates heat, reduces fire.
Calms the central nervous system, relieves anxiety, to fight sleep disturbances, loss of appetite and nervous intestinal complaints.

10.8 Lovage

thermal effect: warm
taste: spicy, bitter
Reduces inner wind and moisture, dissolves stagnation, directs upward, warms Yang, regulates and moves Qi, warms inside, dissolves mucus-cold, eliminates wind-cold.
Stimulates digestion, reduces pain. Extracts of the root are used to flush out urinary tract infections and prevent kidney gravel.

10.9 Lily bulbs

thermal effect: cool
taste: sweet, bitter
Tonifies Yin, soothes Shen / Spirit. Moisturizes the lungs, clears heat and stops coughing.
Calms nerves, good to fight scaly skin. The onions and the petals are added to ointments in the Orient, which can heal muscles and tendons.
White lily (astringent).

10.10 Dandelion (young plants)

thermal effect: cool
taste: sweet, bitter
Cools liver-heat, reduces internal heat, softens knots, eliminates heat, reduces fire, dissolves mucus heat, moves blood, tonifies qi.
Detoxifies, relieves inflammation. Regulates digestion, helps with rheumatism, releases kidney stones, leaves pimples and chronic skin disorders disappear.

10.11 Parsley

thermal effect: warm
taste: bitter
Nourishes blood and liver, harmonizes liver and spleen, strengthens eyesight, preserves juices, contracts. Dissolves moisture and warms Yang.
Stimulates liver function, detoxifies. Forces urinating. Relieves flatulence. Digestive and menstrual stimulating, birth-
accelerating, memory-enhancing, blood-purifying, skin-smoothing.

10.12 Rosemary

thermal effect: warm
taste: bitter
Dries out, leads down. Strengthens the heart, lungs and spleen qi, strengthens liver blood. Strengthens heart-Yin. Expels spleen heat / cold moisture. Strengthens spleen and kidney yang.
Promotes digestion, relieves bloating, strengthens lung, spleen and kidney. Affects the circulation and nerves. Appetizing. Baths help to fight circulatory disorders as well as with gout and rheumatism.

10.13   Sage

thermal effect: neutral
taste: bitter, spicy
Expels slime, guides down, strengthens Qi, eliminates Wind-Heat,
eliminate heat induced by Yin deficiency.
Good to fight yeast infections. The leaves have a digestive effect and are
used in greasy foods. Antiperspirant effect. Helps to relieve coughing
attacks. Dries out.

10.14   Sorrel

thermal effect: cold
taste: sour
Protects the fluids, pull together.
Astringent, hematopoietic, purifies the blood, diuretic. Good to fight liver
weakness, upset stomach, indigestion, constipation, diarrhea, worms,
scurvy, anemia, women's complaints, wounds, skin rashes, boils, ulcers,
swelling.

10.15   Black caraway

thermal effect: warm
taste: spicy, sweet
Dissolve / transform moisture, tonifyes Yang and Qi, moves blood,
suppresses inner wind.
Detoxifying, immunoregulatory. In addition, the oil should stimulate the
formation of bone marrow cells and generally protect body cells from
viruses.

10.16   King Solomon's-seal

thermal effect: neutral
taste: sweet, bitter
Tonifies Yin and Qi, astringent, tonifies blood, eliminates wind-cold / heat-
wetness.
Used to repair wounds or damaged tissue. Good to fight dry cough,
earlier also tuberculosis and dysentery, as well as diarrhea and
hemorrhoids.

10.17 Yam root, yam root tuber

thermal effect: neutral
taste: sweet
Tonifies Yin, Yang and Qi, reduces inner wind, dissolves wetness, warms Yang.
Solves cramps (in the gastrointestinal tract). Digestive through increased bile production. Anti-inflammatory in rheumatic diseases.
Mucolytic agent for coughing. Relief of menopausal symptoms.

11 Basics of Nutrition

The basic principles of nutrition described herein are general recommendations. They are not aimed at a specific form of therapy. Recommendations concerning a therapy have priority.

11.1 Nutrition

Regular meals in a relaxed atmosphere. A warm breakfast is considered a good start into the day.

The main meals ought to be taken for lunch – supper in the early evening. Pay attention to feeling hungry or sated: don't eat too much nor remain hungry is the rule

Prepare the meals freshly from natural, regional products. Frozen, heat-conserved, industrially prepared or foodstuffs cooked in the microwave oven are rejected.

Choice of foodstuffs according to the season: more cooling food in summer, more warming food in winter.

Eat cooked food at least twice a day. Food and drinks ought to be lukewarm, never ice-cold or hot.

Raw vegetables, briefly cooked vegetables, freshly squeezed juices and mineral water are not recommended. Milk and dairy products are only included in the diet if they don't cause problems. Don't use therapeutic recipes over a longer period without consulting your doctor or therapist.

Varied food
Enjoy the diversity of foodstuffs. Characteristics of a balanced nutrition are variety, suitable combination and a balanced quantity of rich and low energy foodstuffs (on one hand avoiding undersupply with essential nutrients and on the other hand to take to many undesirable substances).

A lot of Cereal Products - and Potatoes
Bread, pasta, rice, cereal flakes (best wholemeal) as well as potatoes contain almost no fat, but many vitamins, mineral nutrients, trace elements, roughage and secondary plant substances. These foodstuffs ought to be taken with low-fat side dishes.

Vegetables and Fruit – „Take Five" every day ... 5 portions of vegetables and fruit a day, as fresh as possible, briefly cooked, or maybe one portion as a juice – ideal as a side dish to every meal as well as snack between meals: Thus a lot of vitamins, mineral nutrients as well as roughage and secondary plant substances

Daily milk and dairy products
Milk and Dairy Products every Day, once or twice per Week Fish;
meat, sausages as well as eggs moderately. These foodstuffs contain
valuable nutrients like calcium in the milk, iodine selenium and omega-3
fat acids in saltwater fish. Meat is favorable due to its high content of
disposable iron and the vitamins B1, B6 and B12. Quantities of 300 – 600
g meat and sausage per week are sufficient. Prefer low-fat products,
especially in meat- and dairy products.

Low-fat and fatty Foodstuffs
Fat supplies us with essential fat acids and fatty foodstuffs contain also
fat-soluble vitamins. Fat is high in energy; therefore much fat in the food
may cause overweight, possibly also cancer. Too many saturated fat
acids may further a tendency for cardio-vascular diseases in the long
term. Prefer vegetable oils and fats (e.g. rapeseed-, olive-, soya-oils and
solid fats produced therefrom). Beware of invisible fat in meat- and dairy
products, pastry and sweets as well as in fast-food and convenience
foods. 70 – 90 g fat per day is sufficient.

Moderately Sugar and Salt
Take sugar and foods/drinks containing various kinds of sugar (e.g.
glucose syrup) only occasionally. Use herbs and spices as well as a little
salt creatively. Prefer salt containing iodine.

Plenty of Liquids
Water is absolutely essential. Drink 1-2 l liquids every day. Prefer water
(with or without gas) and other low-calorie drinks. Alcoholic drinks should
not be taken.

Tasty Dishes, carefully cooked
Cook the meals with as low temperatures and as short as possible, using
little water and fat – this preserves the original taste, keeps the nutrients
intact and prevents the production of harmful compounds.

Take time and enjoy the food
Take your Time and enjoy your Food
Eating consciously helps to eat right. The eye enjoys food, too. It's fun,
invites to enjoy varied dishes and stimulates the feeling of satiety.

Watch your Weight and stay in Motion
A balanced diet and a lot of exercise and sport (30 – 60 min/day) are a
healthy combination. The right weight furthers well-being and health.
Thermals, directional effectiveness, digestive power

There are various criteria for judging the effectiveness of herbs and foodstuffs.

The use of certain herbs and ingredients is based on observations of the effects on the body which these foodstuffs, herbs and spices show after having eaten them. The medical science has developed following system: Every ingredient or herb has a directional effectiveness. Furthermore, there are herbs which have a special effect on certain organs.

The basic condition for a healthy metabolism is to obtain sufficient energy from food and that the digestive process doesn't use too much energy. An easily digestible meal makes content and sated, doesn't cause flatulence and fatigue after the meal. The perfect spices increase the healthiness of our meals. Very often, just small doses of herbs and spices will suffice. They are not used to make us sated, but to help our digestive organs to digest the food.

11.2 Recipes

The recipes list the ingredients to be used and the cooking instructions show how the dish is prepared. The list of ingredients shows the concerned quantities as well as the relevance for the therapy. If you find „less than mentioned", try to comply or find an alternative from the „list of recommended foodstuffs". Mostly it shall result just in a small change of taste when you simply avoid this ingredient.

Mild cooking methods: boiling, stewing, poaching, steaming
Strong cooking methods: barbecuing, roasting, frying, smoking
Balanced cooking methods: deep-frying, baking brick
Deep-freezing and warming in the microwave oven should be avoided (denaturalization).

11.3 Foodstuffs

Foodstuffs have an effect on body and soul like medicinal herbs, only a very much milder one. Dietary advice is mainly based on regional foodstuffs. The knowledge about the effects of each foodstuff and the knowledge, when which foodstuff shall be used, is based on the orthodox school of medicine. Use ecologic-organic products, if possible. As everything should be cooked for a long time due to a better digestability and very rarely eaten raw, the food agrees with everyone.

The classification of the foodstuffs according to their effect on the body is the basis in order to achieve a harmonious status of health.

Dietary advisors do not recommend certain foodstuffs for everyone. The individual diet is tailor-made for the individual constitution.

Buy only fresh and ripe fruit and vegetables. You ought to leave unripe fruit and vegetables and such with brown spots and wilted leaves behind in the market. In this case take deep-frozen goods (never ready-to-serve dishes!). Fruit and vegetables are deep-frozen immediately after harvesting and often contain more vitamins and minerals than the goods from the vegetable shelf. Whereas conserved or tinned goods contain very much less biological substances. Also, salt, sugar and others are mostly added to the latter. Never leave the foodstuffs in the water after washing them to avoid that many vital substances get drowned. Clean salads, fruit and vegetables immediately before serving.

Please make sure of the hygienic processing of foodstuffs. Clean your salads, fruit and vegetables carefully. When cooking with meat, prepare all ingredients first and then process the meat products. Clean the worktop and tools very carefully. Wooden surfaces ought to be treated with a mild disinfectant regularly in order to reduce germination.
Store fruit and vegetables separately, if possible. Harvested fruit and vegetables are still alive and emit e.g. ethylene gas, which makes other products ripen and age faster. Keep meat and fish in the closed packaging or store them in the fridge in closed containers.

11.4 Herbs

There are some basic rules for storing medicinal herbs. On principle, herbs must be protected from direct sunlight, humidity and heat.

Containers for the storage of herbs may be glasses, ceramic jars and even plastic containers. However, plastic is a rather unsuitable material and should only be a short-term solution. In case of glass containers, use a dark material.

Medicinal herbs cannot be kept for any long period. The shelf life of herbs is limited. However, it can be prolonged with suitable storage. The place should be dark, rather cool and absolutely dry. A wooden medicine cabinet, placed not directly next to a source of heat, would be ideal. Never buy large quantities of herbs so as not to have to throw them away. Label the container with the name of the herb and the date of harvesting or processing.

12 Other dietic-books

The following syndromes of dietetics, TCM or for a therapy supplement for cancer are available.

Dietetics

E001. Nutrition of the infant - baby food
E002. Nutrition during lactation
E003. Nutrition in old age
E004. Nutrition of children and adolescents
E005. Nutrition of athletes
E006. Light weight
E007. Pregnancy
E008. Full food

Protein and electrolyte - kidneys
E009. (hemodialysis) dialysis treatment
E010. Acute renal failure
E011. Chronic renal insufficiency
E012. Nephrotic syndrome
E013. Kidney stones (nephrolithiasis)

Gastrointestinal tract - pancreas
E014. Acute pancreatitis (inflammation of the pancreas)
E015. Chronic pancreatitis (inflammation of the pancreas)

Gastrointestinal tract - small intestine and large intestine
E016. Acute obstipation (constipation)
E017. Chronic obstipation (constipation)
E018. Colon irritabile
E019. Diverticulitis
E020. Acquired lactose intolerance (lactose malabsorption)
E021. Fructose malabsorption
E022. Glutensensitive enteropathy (celiac disease)
E023. Colectomy
E024. Short Bowel Syndrome

Gastrointestinal tract - liver, gallbladder, bile ducts
E025. Acute and chronic hepatitis (inflammation of the liver)
E026. Cholelithiasis (bile stones)
E027. fatty liver
E028. cirrhosis

Gastrointestinal tract - Stomach and duodenal intestine
E029. Acute gastritis
E030. Chronic gastritis
E031. Stomach bleeding
E032. Ulcus ventriculi and duodenal ulcer
E033. Condition after gastric surgery

Gastrointestinal tract - oral cavity and esophagus
E034. Stomatitis
E035. Esophageal carcinoma (esophageal cancer)
E036. Refluosophagitis (heartburn)

Special diseases
E037. Phenylketonuria (PKU)
E038. Rheumatic joint diseases

Metabolism
E039. Obesity (overweight)
E040. Diabetes mellitus
E041. Eating disorders (underweight)

Fat metabolism
E042. Hypercholesterolaemia (increased cholesterol level)
E043. Hepatic Encephalopathy

Heart and circulation
E044. Arteriosclerosis (arterial calcification)
E045. Heart insufficiency
E046. Hypertension
E047. Hyperuricaemia and gout

Changed nutrient requirements
E048. In case of fever
E049. For malignant diseases
E050. After burns
E051. Radiation and chemotherapy

CANCER
E100. Pancreatic cancer
E101. Bladder cancer
E102. Blood cancer (leukemia)
E103. Breast cancer
E104. Colorectal cancer
E105. Gastric cancer
E106. Kidney cancer
E107. Esophageal cancer

TCM
E200. Bladder - moisture heat in the bladder
E201. Bladder - moisture and cold in the bladder
E202. Bladder - emptiness and cold in the bladder
E203. Large intestine - external cold affects the large intestine
E204. Large intestine - moisture heat in the large intestine
E205. Large intestine - heat blocks the intestine II acute
E206. Large intestine - dryness of the colon
E207. Large intestine - Yang deficiency (cold)
E208. Heart - Blood insufficiency
E209. Heart - Blood stagnation
E210. Heart - Fire
E211. Heart - Hot mucus clogs the heart pores

E212. Heart - Cold mucus clogs the heart pores
E213. Heart - Qi deficiency
E214. Heart - Yang deficiency
E215. Heart - Yin deficiency
E216. Liver - Ascending Liver Yang
E217. Liver - Blood deficiency
E218. Liver - Blood stagnation
E219. Liver - Moisture heat in liver and gall bladder
E220. Liver - Fire
E221. Liver - Gall bladder Qi-Empty
E222. Liver - Cold in the liver meridian
E223. Liver - Qi stagnation
E224. Liver - Wind
E225. Liver - Wind with ascending liver Yang
E226. Liver - Wind with blood anemic
E227. Liver - Wind with extreme heat
E228. Lung - Qi deficiency
E229. Lung - Mucus-moisture in the lungs
E230. Lung - Mucus-heat in the lungs
E231. Lung - Mucus-cold in the lungs
E232. Lung - Dryness of the lungs
E233. Lung - Wind-heat attacks the lungs
E234. Lung - Wind-cold affects the lungs
E235. Lung - Yin deficiency
E236. Stomach - Bloodstagnation
E237. Stomach - Fire
E238. Stomach - Cold with liquid
E239. Stomach - Nutrition stagnation
E240. Stomach - Qi deficiency
E241. Stomach - Rebellious Qi
E242. Stomach - Yin Emptiness
E243. Spleen - Heat and moisture attack the spleen
E244. Spleen - Coldness and moisture affects the spleen
E245. Spleen - Qi deficiency
E246. Spleen - Qi deficiency + Declining spleen Qi
E247. Spleen - Qi deficiency + spleen does not control the blood
E248. Spleen - Yang deficiency
E249. Kidney - Heart and kidney no longer communicate
E250. Kidney - Jing deficiency
E251. Kidney - Kidneys cannot receive the Qi
E252. Kidney - Qi is not stable
E253. Kidney - Yang deficiency
E254. Kidney - Yin deficiency

For further information visit di-book.com.